Inner Work, Outer Glory

KESHA TRIPPETT

Inner Work. Outer Glory.
© 2017 by Kesha Trippett

Publisher's Cataloging-in-Publication Data

Trippett, Kesha, 1980-

All rights reserved.

Scripture quotations marked KJV are from the King James Version.

Scripture quotations marked NKJV are from the New King James Version®. Copyright © 1982 by Thomas Nelson. Used by permission. All rights reserved.

Scripture quotations marked AMP are from THE AMPLIFIED BIBLE, Copyright © 1954, 1958, 1962, 1964, 1965, 1987 by The Lockman Foundation. All rights reserved. Used by permission. (www.Lockman.org).

Scripture quotations marked The Message are from THE MESSAGE. Copyright © by Eugene H. Peterson 1993, 1994, 1995, 1996, 2000, 2001, 2002. Used by permission of Tyndale House Publishers, Inc.

No part of this publication may be reproduced in any form without the prior written permission of the publisher except in the case of brief quotations in articles and reviews.

Published in the United States of America

Cover Photography by Aaron Alston

I dedicate this book to my husband, Bernard Trippett, who has loved me unconditionally during God's inner work in my heart. I pray he will be richly blessed by God's display of glory in my life.

Table of Contents

Foreword by Kristi Jeanine Bell-Jenkins	1
Introduction	3
Chapter 1: God's Inner Work	4
Poem "I Open My Heart"	19
A Word from the Lord " You are a Kingdom Woman"	20
Chapter 2: Lord, Teach Me	22
Poem "It Takes Courage"	34
A Word from the Lord "I Promise You Will Reap"	35
Chapter 3: You Are Being Deeply Rooted	36
Poem "Thank You Lord"	48
A Word from the Lord "My Glory You Will See"	49
Chapter 4: Show Me Your Glory	51
Poem "Until"	59
A Word from the Lord "Believe Me for Greater	61

Chapter 5: The Glory of God	63
Poem "Inspired"	80
A Word from the Lord "There's Nothing Too Hard for Me"	81
Gift of Salvation	83
Renew Your Vow	85
The Gift of Holy Spirit	87
Where Do I Go From Here?	89
Who I Am in Christ Scriptures	93
About the Author	98

FOREWORD

Daughters, sisters, wives, mothers, executives, entrepreneurs, homemakers, pastors, evangelists, and any other position we may hold; as women, we wear these titles, and we serve with a smile. While we juggle our responsibilities well, no one can see the circus that is going on behind closed doors. Yes, we love God with all of our hearts, and our absolute desire is to please Him, but somewhere along the way we got caught up in the day-to-day routine of life, and we began to believe the outcomes of the struggles we've faced. Until one day we look around and ask ourselves, "How in the world did I get here?" And more importantly, "How do I get back?"

Throughout this book, as I read each page, each scripture, and each story, I was in awe of how these words so eloquently expressed feelings, frustrations, and emotions that I never uttered to anyone—not even to God Himself. I cried as I was gently reminded time and time again, that no matter where I was or what was happening in my life, God's answer to me was still…yes! In knowing that "yes," I was reassured that I am still worthy of God's glory. As are you, my dear, dear sister. As are you. You are still crown worthy, and it's your time!

It's your time to hold your head high again. It's your time to return to your first Love. And while you may not understand everything now, it will all make sense with each turn of the page.

Minister Kristi Jeanine Bell-Jenkins

New Birth Christian Ministries, Tennille, GA

INTRODUCTION

As you read this book, I would like for you to examine where you are in your relationship with God. Are you yielding to His inner work in you? Are you being shifted into a new level of faith and glory? Or are you still hiding behind fears, too afraid to yield, too afraid of change, and too afraid to walk in the glory of God? No matter your answer to these questions, I want to help you identify *where* you are, help you learn *who* you are and help you understand *why* you are here.

Within these pages, you will find encouragement, inspiring poems and several divine messages that God has given me to share with you. I believe you will be blessed, and the Lord will strengthen you on your journey. Let Him take you from faith to faith, and from glory to glory.

In His Love,
Kesha Trippett

CHAPTER 1

God's Inner Work

"Therefore, my beloved, as you have always obeyed, not as in my presence only, but now much more in my absence, work out your own salvation with fear and trembling; for it is God who works in you both to will and to do for His good pleasure" Philippians 2:12-14, NKJV.

The inner working of the Holy Spirit in our hearts is what prepares us for our next level of glory. It is a divine work that is invisible to the human eye, and I believe if we could peer into the spiritual realm and see what God is accomplishing in us; we'd be surprised at how destructive it looks and how noisy it sounds. He tears down strongholds, pulls up sin at the root, destroys false belief systems, and utterly demolishes everything the enemy has built in our hearts and minds over the course of our lives. It is the demolition project of the ages.

Yes, it's uncomfortable, but it's necessary that God destroys what's not like Him before He builds anything. It's necessary that He heals our broken hearts and repairs what's leaking before He pours His glory out into our lives and places us in great positions of power and influence (see Mark 2:22). God has our best interest in mind, He has our destiny in mind, and He has the people He has called us to reach in mind.

The Work of the Enemy

"For the weapons of our warfare are not physical [weapons of flesh and blood], but they are mighty before God for the overthrow and destruction of strongholds" 2 Corinthians 10:4, Amplified.

From the time you were a little girl until now, the devil has been diligently working at building strongholds in your mind. Every time you experienced hurt or pain, he sought to build a new structure. Whenever someone betrayed you, he told you that you would never trust anyone ever again. Whenever someone abused you, he told you that you were not worthy of love. With every lie you received as true, he established a new stronghold in your mind. If given enough time, Satan will create an entire network of strongholds that completely distorts your view of everything around you. A stronghold affects how you view God, how you view yourself, and how you view others.

I remember when I was counseling a dear friend; she had reached a point in her life when nothing seemed to be working in her favor. After listening to her for a while, I asked her to tell me every lie the enemy was speaking in her ears. I then lovingly responded to each lie with the truth of God's Word. It was an "Aha" moment for her that I will never forget. She saw how powerful the truth could be, and it was the truth that set her free.

The only way to tear down and completely demolish strongholds is with the truth of God's Word. It's His truth that sets us free, which is why it's important that we establish a relationship with God's Word, by spending time reading our Bible and looking for ways to apply its' principles to our lives. The more truth you receive in your heart, the more it will affect how you view things and how you respond to the challenges you face. When I pray for loved ones, I often pray that God will give them a right view and a right perspective. Perspective is everything! And if you're going to be successful and fulfill your God-given purpose, you definitely will need a right view of God, a right view of yourself and a right view of people.

This part of God's work in us is critical because it sets the stage for what I'm about to share with you next.

When You Find Him, You Find Yourself

I can sit down and take a thousand online self-assessment quizzes that tell me something about myself. They may provide some useful information, but overall, I'll still want to know more. I've discovered only God can tell us who we are and what we are destined to become. He tells us in Psalms 100:3, "...It is He who has made us, and not we ourselves." If He has made us, He knows best the personality, gifts, talents, and purpose He has already placed inside each of us. He knows us best, and the way to discover who we are is by seeking Him. We seek God, not because He is lost to us, but because He is near and we expect to find Him. He says in Jeremiah 29:13 that if we seek Him, we will find Him when we search for Him with all our hearts. When you discover Him, you will discover you. You will see how He's made you, the passion and purpose He's given you, and the gifts He has given you since you were born. All of the pieces will begin to come together. You'll begin to connect the dots, and you will say, "Oh! That's why I do that!"

> *When you discover Him, you will discover you.*

God Will Remind You

Even with learning more about who we are, sometimes we allow negative experiences to change us into someone we're not. I remember when I faced a low point in my life, and I was trying to be someone I wasn't. It made me miserable! I looked up one day and said to myself, "What am I doing? This is not me! This is not Kesha!" We forget who we are because the situation is so painful. That's when we need God to remind us.

The Bible says in Romans 12:1-2 (The Message), "Do not be conformed to this world (this age), [fashioned after and adapted to its external, superficial customs], but be transformed (changed) by the [entire] renewal of your mind [by its new ideals and its new attitude], so that you may prove [for yourselves] what is the good and acceptable and perfect will of God, even the thing which is good and acceptable and perfect [in His sight for you]." What is the good, and acceptable and perfect will of God? I will tell you.

Inner Work, Outer Glory

> *God doesn't want you to be a product of your pain; He wants you to be a product of His glory.*

It is Jesus, and the more we learn to be like Him, the more we please the Father. His goal is that we look like Jesus on the inside and behave like Jesus on the outside. God doesn't want you to be a product of your pain; He wants you to be a product of His glory, a product of His goodness and love, and a product of His grace and mercy. He wants people to look at you and say, "I can tell she's a daughter of God because of how she responds and how she lives her life."

So how does God remind us of who we are when we've forgotten? He places a mirror in front of us (see James 1:23-25). When I went through a time of deep depression and confusion from the enemy, I had completely forgotten who I was and desperately wanted someone to tell me. So one day a friend who I had known for many years called me. You know, God will do that. He will have people call you right when you need it most. So she called me, and I asked her, "Can you please tell me who I am?" She didn't respond the way I thought she'd respond, and honestly, I don't remember what she told me. All I know is that I got off the phone feeling disappointed, thinking to myself, what is the point of having friends if you can't get them to remind you of who you are? But Holy Spirit helped me understand that only He can remind us of who we are. That wasn't her job.

The Bible tells us that Holy Spirit will guide us into all truth and bring all things to our remembrance what the Lord has said to us (see John 16:13, 14:26). The Holy Spirit is the one responsible for reminding us of everything we need to know. I can hear the Lord saying to His people, *"I Am your Maker. I Am the One who made you and formed you. When you need to be reminded of who you are, you need not run to man. Come to Me."*

Maybe you've experienced some difficult trials, and you've forgotten how to be a loving and compassionate person again. Maybe you've forgotten how to be an on fire woman of faith with bold conviction. Maybe you've forgotten, but you can go to your Maker, who is God. The Bible tells us in 2 Corinthians 3:18, when we look to God, we are changed into the same image from glory to glory. When I desperately wanted to remember who I was, I opened my Bible and looked into God's Word, and it was a mirror for my soul. My sister, God's Word will show you who you are! He will show you that you're not what you feel. You are not your past, and you are not your mistakes. You are a chosen daughter of the only true and living God! You are created for His purpose and destined for great things. Look into the mirror of His Word and be reminded by His Holy Spirit of who you are.

Who You Are in Christ

When you are being bombarded left and right with lies from the devil, you must know who you are in Christ. When I was a youth, my pastor instructed me to find everywhere in the New Testament where it said, "In Whom," "In

Him," "In Christ," "Through Him," and "Through Christ." Sadly, I didn't do it until 22 years later when the devil was attacking my identity, and I had nothing to stand on. When the enemy is attacking who you are, if you don't know who you are in Christ, you will lose. The only way to silence him and keep him under your feet where he belongs is by having a full understanding of your identity in Christ.

Trust Him

What does it mean to trust God? It means to place your entire well-being into His hands. It also means you trust in His love for you, and the promises He's made to you. One way He teaches us how to trust in Him is by using older saints to share their stories of how they made it through various challenges.

I once met an older woman who said all throughout her Bible she had written "tried and proven." These words were written next to the scriptures she had stood on in faith and God had

> *No one taught us how to hang in there until we see the morning sun, so we die in the middle of the night.*

proven Himself to be faithful in her life. I believe if we had more women like her sharing their faith, their experiences and teaching younger women how to trust in God, we wouldn't see so many lost and confused women in the church today.

Because there is no passing down of wisdom and no impartations of faith from older saints, women give up on life at the slightest attack from the devil. The smallest amount of persecution or pressure causes many of us to want to quit. I believe it's because we don't know how to go through anything. We don't know how to handle challenges with class. We don't know how to trust God until He brings us out. We don't know how to stand on His promises and watch Him come through for us. We don't know how to walk by faith and not by sight. No one taught us how to hang in there until we see the morning sun, so we die in the middle of the night. We throw in the towel and lose our minds and no longer desire to fight. We desperately need someone to come to our side, rest their hand on our shoulders and say, "Baby, everything is going to be alright. Trust in the Lord. He is faithful, and He will see you through anything."

My sisters, you don't have to lose your mind. You don't have to have a nervous breakdown. You don't have to lose yourself. You can decide right now that you will trust God until He makes a way out of no way for you.

Don't Breakdown, Break Through!

"For in it the righteousness of God is revealed from faith to faith; as it is written, "The just shall live by faith" Romans 1:17, NKJV.

Most often when we hear the word "breakthrough," we think of something we are waiting on God to do. However, did you know

> *At the end of your rope is where you will always find God's grace.*

that you don't have to wait to break through? The moment you decide to get in faith and respond in faith, you are breaking through. The moment you say, "I'm not giving up! I'm going to keep moving forward and trust in my God"; you are breaking through. When everything in you wants to curse, but you praise God instead, you are breaking through! When you are tested in the same way, at the same point by the same evil forces, but this time you say, "No, that's not me anymore!" I'm going to honor God with my life", you are breaking through!

Breakthrough begins the moment you choose to believe and act on God's Word despite how you feel and despite how it looks. At the end of your rope is where you will always find God's grace. And at that moment when you make that key decision to break through, God has a great promotion waiting for you. God has elevation to a new level of faith waiting for you.

It is Well

While the Apostle Paul sat in a Roman prison, he and Silas could have easily sung their songs of praise after they were freed, but God had them sing and write while sitting in a dark dungeon, severely beaten. Some of the best songs, best sermons and best books ever written in the history of humanity were birthed during a great loss or trial.

Horatio Spafford, an American lawyer and Presbyterian church elder, penned the famous American hymn, "It Is Well with My Soul." It was written after the tragic loss of his four daughters in the wreck of the *Ville du Havre* steamship over the Atlantic Ocean after it was by hit an iron vessel. He is said to have written the hymn as he crossed over the same place where his daughters died. If Mr. Spafford were alive today, I believe he would encourage us to know that in Christ, it is well!

Your body may not be well, but all is well in your soul. No matter what you go through in life, remember, it is well. Remember, to not wait until you're free to shout. Shout right now! Sing right now! God will comfort you, and it will then be your responsibility to comfort others with the same comfort He has shown you (see 2 Corinthians 1:4).

I Open My Heart

Lord
my heart is open
enter in
and let it begin
your work within
change what's been
rusting
and gathering
dust
in my heart
my trust
is in you
I need you
to get to the root
I know you're good
and you never would
harm me
so with all that's in me
I give everything to you
change me, God
make me new

A Word from the Lord

"You Are a Kingdom Woman"
November 20, 2015

"Just because you've never done something, doesn't mean you never will, and just because you've always done something, doesn't mean you always will. That Kingdom woman you desire to be, that Kingdom level you desire to operate on, that Kingdom that you desire to help advance, I put that desire in you, and it's waiting for your discovery. All fear, doubt, and unbelief were learned from the experiences you've had here in this earthly realm, but that's not who you are. You are My daughter, and your true identity is in Me. The real you is full of compassion, full of mercy, full of wisdom and affection for Me. Call on Me My beloved and precious daughter, call on Me, and I will surely answer you, and show you great and mighty things that you do not know. I will make you rich in experiences with Me. I will help you see who you are in Me, and who I Am in you. I delivered you from the power of darkness and have placed you in the Kingdom of My dear Son. No one can snatch you from My

Hand. You are Mine, and I am yours. My answer to you is Yes. Yes, you are that Kingdom woman you desire to be in Me. Yes, you will operate on that Kingdom level. Yes, you will advance My Kingdom like you never thought possible. Before you were formed in your mother's womb, I knew you and I called you. I will help you see your greatest potential. I say, Yes."

(Scriptural References: Jeremiah 33:3; Colossians 1:13; Jeremiah 1:5)

CHAPTER 2

LORD, TEACH ME

"But also for this very reason, giving all diligence, add to your faith virtue, to virtue knowledge, to knowledge self-control, to self-control perseverance, to perseverance godliness, to godliness brotherly kindness, and to brotherly kindness love. For if these things are yours and abound, you will be neither barren nor unfruitful in the knowledge of our Lord Jesus Christ." 2 Peter 1:5-8, NKJV.

He Will Teach You to Live by Faith

I'll never forget when God led me to pray and confess several key scriptures over my children. Although we daily covered them in prayer, I felt an unction from the Holy Ghost to confess scriptures over them. I obeyed the Lord and later discovered why He wanted me built up in prayer and His Word.

In March 2009, our four-month-old son was admitted into intensive care for digestive and thyroid issues. He was close to death. I remember the night I followed the ambulance to the children's hospital. I remember praying, *"Lord, not my baby. The devil can't have my baby! Your Word says that the children you have given me are for signs and wonders. You said in your Word that you would pour out your Spirit upon my seed and your blessing upon my offspring. You said my seed would be mighty in the earth."* Every scripture that I had been confessing over the past months was coming up into my heart like ammunition into a gun. I was shooting them out while tears were streaming down my face. God's healing power touched my baby's body, and after three weeks in the hospital, he was totally healed! Praise God!

In that test and trial, God was deepening my faith and was teaching me how to live by faith in His promises. We never know why God allows certain things to occur in our lives, but I can tell you this, if you trust Him no matter the outcome, it will deepen your faith. If you trust Him, it will make you strong, it will astound the unbelieving, and it will glorify your God.

He Will Teach You His Character

I can remember like it was yesterday when my husband and I were dating. One day we had planned to go out to eat after a campus Bible study. Somehow, I overheard him talking to a friend, and I thought he said he'd already gone out to eat with someone else. Feeling upset, I went and ate without him. When Bible Study was over, he asked me if I was ready to go out for dinner. I responded, "No, I already ate, and I'm upset with you!" I shared with him that I overheard his conversation earlier and was upset that he'd go out to eat with someone else when he promised to go out with me. He responded, "What? Why do you think I would do something like that?" I can still remember the look of hurt and disappointment on his face. It hurt him that I didn't trust him enough to know that he'd never make plans with me, and then go and spend time with someone else. It hurt him that I didn't know his character.

It is the same with God. It hurts Him when we don't know His nature, His character, and His heart for us. This is why He wants us to learn of Him. Faith is deeply understanding His nature and trusting in His character. God's inner work will produce in us this kind of faith.

> *Faith is deeply understanding His nature and trusting in His character.*

He Will Teach You How to Wait

There was a time when I volunteered in an elementary art class. The kids were excited to create, and I was happy to assist the teacher. One morning, as the students walked into the classroom and took their seats, the teacher announced we had a new student. Well, the students had already started on a project weeks before, and the new student was behind and needed to be caught up to speed. So I was instructed to take the student to the side and help him.

We sat down, and I could tell he was very eager to start creating. I explained to him what we were about to do, and he nodded to show he understood me. I told him to draw one line on the paper. He drew a line, and then, drew some more lines that I didn't tell him to draw. I realized he was so eager that he was going ahead of me and doing whatever he wanted to do. It became such a problem that we had to trash the first paper and start over. So I looked him in the eyes and said, "I know you are excited about drawing, but to complete this project the way the teacher wants it done, I'm going to need you to listen and wait for my instructions." He nodded.

In life, we can be much like that new student. We are very eager to do everything God has called us to do, but to complete His assignment for our lives, we are going to have to listen and wait for His instructions. We can't get ahead of God thinking we know everything. Yes, you may be eager, but you have to listen to God's step-by-step instructions and follow them. Don't get ahead of God. Stay right in step with Him, and you will reach His glorious destination for your life.

He Will Teach You How to Love Yourself

How much do you love yourself? No, I'm not talking about being a lover *of* self. The Bible clearly warns against that (see 2 Timothy 3:1-2). I'm talking about loving and valuing yourself enough to not stay in an abusive relationship. I'm talking about loving yourself enough to forgive your own mistakes and receive God's love and forgiveness. I'm talking about the kind of love that causes you to wrap your arms around yourself tightly and say, "Girl, everything is going to be alright!" That's loving you. God pours into our empty and depraved hearts His immense love even though we don't deserve it, and when we receive His love, we are now able to give it away. You will never be able to love others properly until you first love you.

He Will Teach You How to Love Others

How much do you care about the lost? How much does your heart break for the sick and hurting? How much do you care for the least of these? As God performs His work in your heart, He will increase your capacity to love others unconditionally. He knows apart from Him; we all love handicapped. We may try to forgive, but we can't forgive anyone without His grace. We try to love the unlovable, but we find it impossible to do. Our human love only goes so far. It's selective and is nothing like what comes from above. It's all talk and no show. Knowing this should make us run to God, desperate to be filled with His love and be taught how to walk in it.

> *You will never be able to love others properly until you first love you.*

Inner Work, Outer Glory

    I would like for you to think of three people in your life you have had the most difficult time loving and forgiving.

Please write those three names down:

1. _____

2. _____

3. _____

    I want you to know that as you yield to God's inner work in your life, God is going to open your eyes to see the individuals that you listed with the eyes of Jesus. You're going to see Him help you forgive. I challenge you to revisit your list of names often and pray over each person fervently from a heartfelt place. You will watch God do something supernatural in you. That person may never change, but God will have changed you, and the power that person had over you and your emotions will be removed. It's the powerful inner working of the Holy Spirit that will set you free.

Remember, no matter how generous you are, how powerful you can pray, or how much you can run and shout, if you don't have love in your heart, my sister, it's all for nothing. If you don't know how to treat people the way you would want to be treated, it's all for nothing. If you want to be great in God's Kingdom, you must learn how to walk in love.

> *If you want to be great in God's Kingdom, you must learn how to walk in love.*

Here is a description of what real love is:

"Love is patient and kind. Love is not jealous or boastful or proud or rude. It does not demand its own way. It is not irritable, and it keeps no record of being wronged. It does not rejoice about injustice but rejoices whenever the truth wins out. Love never gives up, never loses faith, is always hopeful, and endures

through every circumstance" 1 Corinthians 13:4-7, NLT.

He Will Teach You to Be Courageous

God wants to make you into a courageous woman. It doesn't mean you will never feel afraid ever again, but even in the midst of fear, you will obey God. That, my friend, is courage. It is following God no matter how afraid you feel because you know God loves you and will never let you down.

> *"Courage comes from a heart that is CONVINCED it is loved"*
> – Beth Moore

I remember when my husband and I went skydiving for the first time. My mother was so afraid for us that she asked if whether we wanted to give her power of attorney of our children just in case we didn't survive the jump. I remember laughing out loud and reassuring her that she had nothing to worry about. When we arrived on site, we received a quick course on how to skydive, then they strapped us in our harness, and we got on the plane. As we climbed higher and higher in altitude, with our skydiving instructor hooked onto our backs, I remember thinking, "What in the world am I doing?!" But there was no turning back now. I pretended to be brave, but on the inside I was scared. They opened the door to the plane, and my instructor yelled, "It's time!" He began to push me forward in the way someone who has jumped a million times would. I got to the edge of the door, and he said, "Jump!" I took a deep breath, moved forward and rolled out of the plane into the wide open air. Then my instructor noticed I was holding on to my harness (for dear life) instead of spreading my arms like an eagle. So he tapped my hands and out went my arms. I was flying!

You can decide today that you are not going to be ruled by fear another day in your life. You can decide today to accept what the Spirit of the Lord is challenging you to do. You can face the fears in your life head on with God's help. It is not God's will that any of His people live in torment to fear (see 1 John 4:18). It is His will that we live in His rest and His perfect peace. To do this, we must make it a habit of casting down vain imaginations (see 2 Corinthians 10:5). I like to call them crazy imaginations. You know the images the enemy brings to your mind of you or your children becoming sick and dying, or images of you failing miserably. Those images can cause us to experience fear and dread when nothing has happened. God says, cast those vain and empty imaginations down! They are empty because they have no truth in them. They are a lie from the pit of hell. The Lord tells us to take every thought captive in the obedience of Christ. Instead of letting fearful thoughts roam freely in our minds, God tells us to take them captive.

The amazing thing about God is the more you grow in Him, the more He will challenge you. He will help you confront every fear. He will have you do something you've never done and will instruct you to step out on faith in ways you never have before—all to teach you how to live by faith instead of fear.

It Takes Courage

It takes courage
to tell the truth
to follow your heart
to do something alone
to make yourself vulnerable
to leave a longtime love
to trust again
to speak up
to wait on God's best
to start something new
to admit your own ignorance
to believe things will change
to give expecting nothing in return
to be yourself

A WORD FROM THE LORD

"I Promise You Will Reap"
February 12, 2016

"Don't get weary of doing what is right. I promise you will reap. No seed you sow is ever wasted. No prayer you pray is ever in vain. No submitting to My will ever goes unnoticed. Everything you do produces a result. You always reap more than the seed you've sown. The harvest is always greater than the one act of obedience to Me. Keep sowing to the Spirit. Keep doing what pleases Me. Keep siding with Me and what I want. Keep praying. Keep fasting. Keeping fighting the good fight of faith. Keep growing. Keep standing. Keep honoring those whom I have honored. Keep loving those I love. Keep being about unity, about love, and about advancing My Kingdom to the farthest ends of the earth. You will reap, says the Lord."

Scripture References: Genesis 8:22; Psalms 126:5-6

CHAPTER 3

You are Being Deeply Rooted

"As you therefore have received Christ Jesus the Lord, so walk in Him, rooted and built up in Him and established in the faith, as you have been taught, abounding in it with thanksgiving" Colossians 2:6-7, NKJV.

Even though we are rooted and grounded in our knowledge of God, the enemy stops at nothing to try to uproot us. However, he quickly finds that it is not an easy task. Deep down there are things that we know. Deep down we know there is a God and that He loves us. Deep down we know that He will never leave us nor forsake us. Deep down we know that He has chosen us for His divine purposes and plans. Deep down we know that we are redeemed by the precious blood of Jesus and have been made new. This is what being rooted and grounded means—

holding on with everything we have, to what we know deep down.

Let us not uproot and give up! We must hold on and become even more rooted and grounded, and fully convinced of God's love. We must let His Words permeate our heart and soul to the very core of who we are. When we do this, we will see the enemy will not be able to win in our lives. Through Jesus Christ, we are victorious! We are overcomers! We are champions! God is greater than anything we will ever face in this life, and with His help, we can do all things!

Yield

"My little children, for whom I labor in birth again until Christ is formed in you" Galatians 4:19, NKJV.

From the moment you receive Jesus as Savior and Lord of your life, His Spirit comes in and goes to work in changing you from the inside out. However, we can slow down the process by not yielding.

When you go to the dentist, they instruct you to sit down and open your mouth so they can examine your teeth. If you refuse to cooperate, a visit that was only supposed to last 25 minutes could easily turn into an all day appointment. The length of the procedure depends on the cooperation of the patient. It is the same as when someone who is newly saved comes into the faith and completely yields themselves to God. The next thing you know, God is being glorified in their lives in a great way, and they are running with purpose and passion. They are living like Jesus, walking like Jesus, and doing the works of Jesus, and they've only been saved for 12 months. How is that possible when you have people who have been saved for 50 years, and you don't see any growth or visible fruit in their lives? It is a matter of yielding to God and cooperating with His Holy Spirit. Some believers are completely yielded to God, while others are not.

When I pray for my brothers and sisters in Christ, I spend the majority of time praying for them to yield to the Holy Spirit. I know God is going to do His part; we just need to cooperate with Him and do what He's instructing us to do.

Change

Many of us demand change in people's behaviors, but we forget at the root of every behavior is something in the heart that must be dealt with first. There have been many times in my marriage when my husband would ask me to stop doing something that was bothering him. Instead of complaining to me about it, he would simply pray in his personal time with God. I could tell he was praying for me about those areas because God would begin dealing with me and the next thing you know, I begin to change. Prayer works!

The inner work of the Lord not only applies to our lives, but to those we love and care about as well. Before you go on a rampage and begin to attack someone's behavior, let God get to the heart of the matter and minister to the root. Someone could easily change for a brief moment just so you can shut up and stop complaining, then a few weeks will go by, and they're back to doing the same old things that drove you crazy. We need God to get to the root of the problem, and that root is in their heart and mind.

We look at outward appearances and behaviors, while God clearly sees right into our hearts (see 1 Samuel 16:7). So pray to Him and move out the way. He didn't call you to perform the inner work in your spouse, in your children, in your relatives, or anyone else. He is the One that does it. He knows the adjustments that need to be made to bring about His kind of results. Don't take it upon yourself to try to change people, because the truth is, we have a hard enough time trying to change ourselves. If you trust God and apply your faith, God's anointing and power will do all the heavy lifting, changing, healing and delivering. Remember, it's not by your might or power, it's by His Spirit (see Zechariah 4:6).

> *God is the only One that knows how to change the heart.*

Grow

"I am the vine, you are the branches. He who abides in Me, and I in him, bears much fruit; for without Me you can do nothing" John 15:5, NKJV.

Jesus said apart from Him we can do nothing. We can do no great works without Him. I'm reminded of a great man of faith, Hudson Taylor, who founded the China Inland Mission, a great evangelistic missionary work in China. His ministry was responsible for bringing 800 missionaries into China, in which they started 125 schools that resulted in the salvation of 18,000 people. In reading his amazing story, I was moved when I saw the correlation between God's inner work in his heart and the lasting work he was used to do in that country. Notice I said "lasting work." Only what we do for God's Kingdom will last.

Consider the mighty oak tree. Though it reaches 60 to 100 ft in the sky and has branches that spread 150 ft across, hidden beneath the earth's surface is a complex root system that's deep and wide. God wants our knowledge of His Word to develop a complex root system in our heart like the mighty oak tree. This is what makes us unmovable. He desires that we grow in Him, but growth is first downward.

One day I asked God why I wasn't growing. To me, growth meant you're going higher and higher. He then spoke to my heart, "You are growing. You're growing downward." My friend, you may not see any progress at all in your life, but God does. He sees your roots wrapping around Him and aligning with Him. He sees you looking for ways to apply His Word and your knowledge of Him deepening. God sees this beautiful process taking place in your heart long before you see anything above the surface. He tells us in John 12:24, *"Most assuredly, I say to you, unless a grain of wheat falls into the ground and dies, it remains alone; but if it dies, it produces much grain."* Keep growing downward. Soon you will break through the hard earth, and you will reach high and stretch wide in helping others.

Don't be concerned with how high you go, rather focus on how deep you go in your understanding of the Lord. You don't have to prove anything; it is God that proves you. He warns us in Jeremiah 9:23-24 (NKJV), *"Let not the wise man glory in his wisdom, let not the mighty man glory in his might, nor let the rich man glory in his riches; but let him who glories glory in this, that he understands and knows Me, that I am the LORD, exercising lovingkindness, judgment, and righteousness in the earth. For in these I delight, says the LORD."* God may have given you great strength, great wisdom, or great riches, but don't glory in it. None of these make you who you are. If you're going to brag or glory about anything, glory in the fact that you know and understand the Lord. Talk about your roots that are completely established in Him!

People may admire you for your strength, your wisdom, or your money, but never think that's all you have going for yourself. There's more to you than what meets the eye. It is our relationship with God that makes us somebody, and that is something that can never be taken from us. When you possess that knowledge, it makes you strong and powerful.

He Does It, Not You

The Bible says, *"He who calls you is faithful, who also will do it" (see* 1 Thessalonians 5:24, NKJV). God has encouraged me many, many times with this Scripture. We have to know that the same God who called us, is the same God who will also do it. Everything He does in you, He will do through you. He will free you, and free others through you. He will heal you and will heal others through you. He will be good to you and will be good to others through you. So if this is the case, we can boldly say, "Yes Lord, have your way in me because I know whatever you do in me, you're going to do through me."

Knowing this alone should remove all of the pressure you may place on yourself. It is God who will accomplish this great work in and through you, and all He needs is your cooperation.

It's an Ongoing Process

There were approximately fifteen years between the time it was revealed to David that he would be king of Israel, and the day he was crowned. However, even in the glory of being king, David's character was still being developed through the things he endured. There were forty years between the time it was revealed to Moses that he would deliver God's people from Egyptian slavery, and the day he stepped into that calling. However, even in the glory of parting the Red Sea and watching manna fall fresh from heaven, Moses was still being worked on by the Lord. You see, God is never done with us. He is always working, always pruning, and always refining us so we can shine ever brighter and produce more fruit for His glory.

Never think that God's work in you is a one-time thing. Let me tell you; it's not. God will continue to work in our hearts until we breathe our very last breath.

Thank Him

"In everything give thanks; for this is the will of God in Christ Jesus for you" 1 Thessalonians 5:18, NKJV.

I remember when we had a new home with no furniture to sit on. Instead of murmuring and complaining, we called our four young children into our empty living room and explained that we were going to praise God as a family. So we shouted, lifted our voices and praised God with everything we had. Two weeks later, our living room was full of furniture.

God honors us when we honor Him and He blesses us when we bless Him. He loves the sound of our voices. He loves the sound of our steps on the floor and the clap of our hands. He lives in our praises. I want you to pause from reading for a moment to thank God. Thank Him for loving you just how you are, but caring enough to not let you stay how you are. Thank Him for changing you from the inside out. Thank Him for His correction and His rebukes. Thank Him for His love and grace. Thank Him for His inner work in your life!

Thank You Lord

Thank you
for the storm
it keeps my arms raised
thank you
for the trial
it keeps me on my face
and for the test
it keeps me
seeking
searching
and knocking
Lord I want more of you
humble me
remind me
that more of you
will cost all of me

A WORD FROM THE LORD

"My Glory You Will See"
August 27, 2014

"You will see My mighty fist and My strong muscle displayed in your life like never before. You have wanted to see My glory. From your spirit, you cried, "Lord show me Your glory." So My glory you will see. You have waited, and now the vision speaks. Now My dream for you will come to pass. The place I have brought you to, no one will be able to separate you from it. The place My love has brought you to, no one can rob you of it. And what my love has taught you, no one can cause you to unlearn it. It's yours. Rejoice in the land of the living! Rejoice in My deliverance and in My special care of you. Rejoice that you know and understand My love, My character and My nature to bless those who diligently seek Me. This is a time of seeing what I have longed for you to see, tasting what I have longed for you to taste, and receiving what I have longed to give you. It is a time of great and

tremendous rejoicing on your part and great action and power on Mine. Says the Spirit of the Lord."

Scriptural References: Psalms 63:2; Psalms 27:13; 2 Timothy 3:14; Hebrews 11:6

CHAPTER 4
SHOW ME YOUR GLORY

I had been praying for God to show me His glory, and to show Himself strong in my life. He spoke the word you just read to me during a time when I was fighting with everything in me to break free of depression. I was fighting for my future and God's purpose for my life. I was fighting for my children to have a mommy that was present. I was fighting for my husband to have a wife that was no longer tormented by fear. I was in the fight of my life and just as God came to the prophet Elijah as he hid in a cave, He was coming to me to let me know, *"You have wanted to see My glory...So My glory you will see* (see 1 Kings 19:13)." He came to me in a still small voice and told me what shall be. God has a special way of speaking light into our darkness all with one word and completely silencing the voice of the enemy. He will send His Word to lift your head.

He will send His Word to heal your hurt and pain (see Psalms 107:20). He will send His Word and put the wind back in your sail. His Word never returns to Him without accomplishing His desired result.

God spoke to me when I was desperate to see Him move. For years, I had seen people shout and run around, but never receive a breakthrough. I watched them pray, but never receive the promise. I wanted to know the God that parted the Red Sea. I wanted to know the God that had filled the house with a cloud of glory, and no one could stand to minister. I was longing to know the God that caused fire to fall from heaven before the 450 prophets of Baal and the 400 prophets of Asherah. Where was the God that I had read about while growing up in church and had heard preached countless of times? Where was His glory in our modern world? Had He gone on vacation? I refused to believe He was absent when He says He is with us always. If He is with us, His glory is also with us.

Let Him Shift You

I believe it is God's desire that we walk in His glory every day of our lives. We know how to suffer, but we also must learn how to reign in Christ.

When Moses asked God to show him His glory, the Lord hid him in the cleft of a rock, and then the glory of the Lord passed by him, showing Moses His backside. He changed Moses' position (see Exodus 33:18-23). In order to see God's glory in your life, you must let God change your position. This is no time to choose comfort over divine positioning in God. This is no time to choose to stay in your favorite place, with your favorite people, eating your favorite meals. Let God show you a better view. Let Him shift you.

I remember when I learned a valuable lesson when I first started Daughters of the King International Ministries. It felt as though I was connected to a spout of wisdom and revelation, and it was pouring out into my heart profusely. It was like I was tuned into the frequency of the

Holy Ghost and there was no static. I couldn't write down all of the revelations; they were pouring out so fast. So in my excitement, I called a friend to ask if she was also experiencing this kind of connection to God in her life. She said, no. I thought she was going to say, "Yes my sister, I'm experiencing the same thing! Isn't it awesome?!" I had made a mistake many of us make when we're new to walking in the glory of God. I thought everyone was experiencing the same thing when in reality, everyone isn't. It's not that they can't, but they haven't let God shift them. He was showing me how to walk in His glory even when those I love and care about choose to remain where they are.

God wants us to continue loving on people, to keep shining, keep trusting Him, and keep holding up the blood-stained banner of Jesus Christ. It's God that enlightens minds and gives understanding where there is none.

Reign with Him

"If we suffer, we shall also reign with him: if we deny him, he also will deny us" 2 Timothy 2:12, KJV.

God is not a harsh taskmaster. He will never let the pain of your past outweigh His glorious future for your life. He *is* a rewarder of them that diligently seek Him. He *is* a rewarder of those who refuse to cast away their confidence in Him. He *is* a rewarder of those who live right before Him. Yes, He is!

Many people think all Christians do is suffer, suffer, suffer, but I read in my Bible that when we suffer with Him, we will also reign with Him. It is God's will that you reign, reign, reign! Yes, we should want to know Him and the fellowship of His suffering, but we should also desire to walk in the power of His resurrection and the victorious life Jesus purchased for us with His precious blood.

Affliction produces glory, it launches ministries, it authors books, and it inspires songs and gives powerful revelation and insight. If the devil only knew how God would be glorified in your life, he would have left you alone! Let God produce great glory from all you've been through (see Romans 8:30). Don't suffer and not reign! Don't be tested and not testify! Don't be pressed unimaginably and not shine with God's glorious light! Don't let the enemy get off that easy! It is your time to shine and let the Father be glorified in your life!

God is Right About You

When it comes time for God to be glorified through you, you may wonder if you're ready. You may ask yourself; do I know enough of my Bible to be effective? Is my relationship with God strong enough to handle all that comes with success? What if I fail? All of these questions plagued my mind when God called me and I began to "walk on water". I didn't think I was ready at all. I kept asking God, "Are you sure you called the right person?" I could think of a long list of people who I felt were far more qualified and far more capable to handle all that comes with being in my position. I felt unsure, but I went along with it anyway because deep within my heart I wanted God to be right about me.

No matter how afraid you may be of the success and glory God has waiting for you, He will show you that He is right about you. Think about that for a moment. God is right about *you*. That truth alone is a heart-full. God knows you better than you know yourself, and He has spoken what you will be and the purpose you will fulfill in the earth. He has said what He will do in and through you, and what great influence you will have for His glory. And guess what? He is right! You may not see it fully, but you have to look

> *No matter how afraid you may be of the success and glory God has waiting for you, He will show you that He is right about you.*

through the lens of grace. Look at yourself in the mirror and declare, "Everything God has said about me is true! God is right about me!" That should give you a huge boost of confidence and put an end to all of the questioning going on in your mind.

You may not be perfect, but you can be perfectly yielded to God. That's all He wants from you. You may not have it all together, but God does. He didn't call you because He thought you had it all together. He called you because He loves you and He loves every person He's predestined for you to reach. He has ordered your steps and He will help you walk in the steps He's laid before you. He will be glorified in your life!

Until

I don't know
the power of God's love
until I make
a complete mess of things
I don't know
the power of God's light
until I walk
through the darkest valley
I don't know
God to be faithful and true
until someone I love
leaves me
I don't fully realize
He lives in me
until I am pressed
unimaginably
it is my sufferings
that help me see
His glory
it is my experiences
that causes my faith

Inner Work, Outer Glory

to grow
it is not my light
that makes me beautiful
it is my struggle
and my determination
to not let
my light die

A Word from the Lord

"Believe Me for Greater"
November 15, 2015

"Learn of Me and get to know My character, My nature and My will for you. Don't you know I care for you deeply and will provide your every need right when you need it? Don't you know it's nothing for Me to provide for you? Don't you know it's nothing for Me to supply you with a car, a house, a husband to love and take care of you? Have not I said, it pleases Me that you prosper and be in health, even as your soul prospers? Have not I said, it is My pleasure to give you the Kingdom? Have not I said, if you seek Me and My Kingdom first and My righteousness, all of these things would be added to you? You have made your requests of Me, and now My most precious daughter, I make My request of you. Ask Me for greater. Ask Me for the heathen. Ask Me to give you the nations. Ask Me to work through you mightily to change the world. Ask Me to be glorified in your life.

Ask Me to bring revival to your city, town, and province. Use your faith to believe Me for greater. Says the Lord."

Scripture References: 3 John 1:2; Luke 12:32; Psalm 2:8; Philippians 4:19; Matthew 6:33

CHAPTER 5

The Glory of God

"To them, God willed to make known what are the riches of the glory of this mystery among the Gentiles: which is Christ in you, the hope of glory."
2 Corinthians 4:17, NKJV.

My first encounter with God's presence was on October 20, 1992. I was twelve years old, and I had reluctantly gone to a church revival with my mother, older brother, and younger sister. The church was packed with several hundreds of people, and I sat two rows behind the pulpit. A traveling evangelist, Dr. Juanita Bynum, entered the sanctuary and began to preach. As she preached, something began to happen, and it was more powerful than anything I had ever experienced. People began to lift their hands and shout out words into the open air. I had never formally met the one they were talking to, but I had a feeling I was about to meet Him for myself. That's when I felt a loving presence surround me. I didn't know anything about God, but I knew I needed to respond. So I imitated those around me, raised my hands high above my head and began to say, "Thank you Lord" and "Hallelujah." The next thing I know, tears began to pour down my face, and I was worshipping God for the first time in my life. The evangelist then pointed to me and told me to come up front. She said she sensed the anointing on some children. She then laid her hand on my head, and I was on the floor, slain in the Spirit, for the first time. It was a night of several firsts for me, and my life would never be the same.

> *The glory of God brings heaven to earth.*

People ask, what is the glory of God? The glory is God's manifest presence. All of the miracles Jesus did while on earth were manifestations of the glory of God and demonstrations of His Spirit and power—from feeding 5000 plus people to healing the multitudes of all manner of sicknesses and diseases. The glory of God brings heaven to earth. Since there is no sickness in God, He manifests His healing power to remove sickness among us. Since there is no poverty in God, He manifests supernatural provision. Since there is no bondage where God is, He manifests deliverance and total freedom. He works through anyone who is yielded to Him and manifests His glory and power.

Welcome Holy Spirit

God wants you to operate in His power. This is why I believe it's so important that every believer receives the baptism of the Holy Ghost with the Bible evidence of speaking in other tongues (see Acts 1:8, 2:4). When you pray in tongues, it reminds you that God lives in you. The Bible says the Holy Spirit bears witness with our spirit that we are children of God (see Romans 8:16). There are many powerless churches today because they aren't letting the

Holy Spirit have His way. They're kicking Him out of their lives and out of their churches. We must invite the Holy Spirit back into our lives. We must welcome Him back into our gatherings and let Him have free course. He wants to perform many miracles that will bring the lost flooding through the doors.

When Jesus was at the wedding feast, and they had run out of wine, Jesus performed His first miracle in which He turned water into the best wine they'd ever tasted. The Bible tells us, *"This beginning of signs Jesus did in Cana of Galilee, and manifested His glory; and His disciples believed in Him"* (see John 2:11, NKJV).

I want you to know today by the Spirit of God that you will yield to God and He will use you mightily, and it will be the beginning of miracles. It will be the beginning of revival. It will be the beginning of a great awakening and great deliverance. He will manifest His glory through you and those around you will see His glory and will believe on Him. They will know it is not you; it is God working through you.

Whatever capacity He has used you in before, don't think that is all God is going to do. No, there's more! Far more! It's only the beginning! So stay the course, my sister. Stay focused, and you will watch God take you from faith to faith and from glory to glory until you enter into eternal glory. You will receive an entrance into God's eternal Kingdom. You will receive a crown of life. You will receive a great reward from our Father!

Understand Who Lives in You

"But we have this treasure in earthen vessels, so that the surpassing greatness of the power will be of God and not from ourselves…" 2 Corinthians 4:7, NKJV

While sitting in a restaurant one day, I looked around desiring to bless someone by paying for their meal. Because I knew I had money in the bank, I was confident that I could be used by God to be a blessing. When you know who lives on the inside of you, you can be confident that God can use you to be a blessing in someone's life.

You have the Spirit of the Lord residing within you. The Bible also calls Him the Spirit of Glory, and He lives in you (see 1 Peter 4:14). God wants to use you to set people free. He wants to use you to bring repentance and healing to nations. Great revivals and movements in history were sparked by those who were fully persuaded that God lived in them. They walked in the glory of God, and that glory produced visible and tangible results.

When you know who lives within you, you can command light to shine in a dark place. You can command cancer to leave someone's body. You can command Satan to take his hands off of your loved ones and command that they are loosed from their bondage. You can walk in the love of God and in the power God like never before.

It is Jesus that does the work through you as you lay down your life. He picks it up and lives through you.

God's Glory Will Make You Shine

"Let your light so shine before men, that they may see your good works and glorify your Father in heaven."
Matthew 5:16, NKJV

God loves you, and He has lavishly poured out His love into your heart and has filled you with His Holy Spirit. You are blessed, and many others will be blessed by watching how you shine brightly for Him. They will see your good works and glorify the Lord. This is why it is important that you stay humble and stay mindful of your behavior before those who do not know Him. Show the genuine love of Jesus. Walk in the joy of the Lord. Live in the peace of His Spirit. Walk in self-control. Be good. Be patient. Have faith. Whether you are on the mountaintop, or in the valley low, be steadfast, unmovable, always abounding in the work of the Lord, because you know your labor in Him is not in vain. God is using your light and your witness to draw many, many people to Him.

Do you now see how great a role you have in the building of His kingdom? It's no small task He's assigned you. You are important to God. You are important to your generation. Don't relax your hold on Him. Don't draw back in fear. Don't give up and don't give out. Even when you face the most difficult trials of your life, that walking in glory are sure to bring; please remember your witness. The Apostle Paul said in 2 Timothy 2:10, "Therefore I endure all things for the sake of the elect, that they also may obtain the salvation which is in Christ Jesus with eternal glory." Like Jesus, he chose to endure the hardships, the beatings, the imprisonments, the great distress, the ridicule and the persecution. He endured it for every person who was destined to be reached through him.

There are people around you that are destined to be in God's kingdom. There are people watching your life that are destined to be Holy Ghost-filled saints of God. Endure all things. See many people won to Jesus because they experienced God's love in you. Let that be the joy that you set before you. Endure all things for their sake. Sustain under pressure without breaking, for their sakes. Win in life and stay humble, for their sakes. Refuse to give in to the temptations of the enemy, for their sake. Persevere to the end, giving God everything you've got, for their sake. Be constantly aware of your witness to the world, not merely your words, but how you live your life before them.

God's Glory Will Bring You Wealth

If you want to carry God's glory while you remain in poverty, sorry, you will be sadly mistaken. People who carry God's glory walk in favor, they walk in wealth and prosperity. Everything they touch prospers! As we find in Isaiah 60:5, the Lord will cause the abundance of the sea to be turned to you and the wealth of the nations to come to you. There will be a large transfer of wealth into your hands, and God wants you to use it for the expansion of His Kingdom.

The Bible calls wealth, "force". Poverty causes you to have no force to create change in the world. Wealth, however, is a powerful force, which is why God wants it in the hands of His people so that we can further the gospel and occupy till He comes.

God's Glory Will Produce Miracles

The glory of God will produce miracles through you that will cause many to believe. Jesus performed so many miracles within the space of three years of ministry that all of the books in the world cannot contain them (see John 21:25)! The same anointing that rested on Him rests on you. That same mighty power has been given to you. Our responsibility is to allow God's glory to flow through us to produce all kinds of miracles in people's lives. This will get the world's attention and can cause many to repent and turn to God.

God's Glory Reveals Who You Are

The whole earth groans and waits in great expectation for the sons of God to be revealed (see Romans 8:19). Who are His sons? These are men and women in the earth who have chosen not to bow their knee to the enemy. In this hour, I believe God is revealing who truly belongs to Him and who doesn't. Who is for Him and who is against Him. He is separating the real believers from the wolves in sheep clothing. Everyone who calls Him Father isn't His child and everyone who calls themselves a Christian does not love Him. God knows who belongs to Him and He is getting ready to reveal them in the earth, in every nation, and every place.

God's Glory Will Provide

"And my God shall supply all your need according to His riches in glory by Christ Jesus" Philippians 4:19, KJV.

As a mother that nurses our four-month-old son frequently throughout the day, it's a blessing to know anytime he's hungry or thirsty; he can latch on and receive a rich and abundant supply of milk. The Lord began to show me how He also has an abundant supply of riches in His glory. Every born-again believer has access to God's abundant supply twenty-four hours a day, seven days a week. Anything we could ever need is found in His glory: wisdom, strength, deliverance, healing, knowledge, and understanding, peace, increase, and favor. He supplies all our need according to His riches in glory, and that's a good thing because if it were according to our riches, we would be in terrible shape.

One morning while talking with my husband, I shared with him how I wanted to know where and how God would bring wealth into our lives. I knew what we had in the spirit, but I was beginning to feel impatient. So my husband encouraged me, and we began to pray. As we prayed, the Lord spoke to me, "Don't say any more, Where is it? Or, how is it? Just thank

Me. My glory is all around you." Immediately I got down on my knees and asked God to forgive me. Instead of murmuring and complaining, I changed my words to, "Thank you, God! Your glory surrounds me!" God doesn't like when we complain. He wants us to trust Him. Everything we need is already provided. It's already in our hands. We simply have to do what God is telling us to do and we will see Him manifest wealth in our lives.

God's Glory Will Set You Free

"Now the Lord is the Spirit; and where the Spirit of the Lord is, there is liberty."
2 Corinthians 3:17, NKJV

There is freedom in the Lord. No spirit of oppression, suppression, depression or repression has any right to hold us when God's Spirit has set us free. I'm here to tell you that you can be free to live the life God has called us to live. You can be free to be yourself in Him. Be free to let God take you as high, as far, and as deep as He wants to take you. Be free to live without fear because you know who you are, and what you have on the inside of you.

Point of Decision

There's more to life than what you've been experiencing, but you won't be able to do anything God has purposed you to do while standing in your old familiar place. God is calling you out into the deep. He is challenging you to step out in faith, and He is calling you to totally lose yourself in Him. So what will it be? Let the grace of God challenge you to do what you have never done before. Let the Spirit of Grace help you be all that God created you to be. Let Him inspire you, motivate you, and be your greatest source of encouragement. He will teach you everything you need to know. Side with Him and trust His leading.

I remember when a good friend of mine who served faithfully on my ministry team had to move on. I had learned by then that you couldn't hold on to people when they too have a purpose to fulfill. As we were congratulating her on moving forward into her purpose with her husband, I felt scared to go on without her. She served Daughters of the King in a spirit of excellence as if it was a full-time job for her, she helped hold up my hands when they became tired, and she was just a great source of love and support for me. So, you can imagine when she left, I didn't know what to do.

I remember that Sunday I went to church desperately wanting God to comfort me and reassure me that everything would be ok. When it came time to go to the altar for prayer, I walked up and stood in front of a minister. I remember telling him that a dear friend and team member in my ministry had moved on and I felt like I couldn't do this without her. I admitted that I felt scared. The minister, who was an older man, prayed for me as I cried like a baby. Then he looked me in my eyes and said, "Your walk is going to turn into a pace, and your pace is going to turn into a run." Then he said it again…and again. Those words have stuck with me through the years, and now, by the grace of God, I am running for God. He is the only one I depend on. Everyone could leave me today, but I will still fulfill God's purpose and plan for my life because I know He is with me. We are to put our total confidence in the Lord, not man. Thank God for help, thank God for the support He gives us, but He alone is our God.

Have you ever seen a baby walk for the first time? They eventually grow and let go of their mommy or daddy's hand as they begin to walk. When God said we are to walk by faith and not by sight, this is the image that comes to my mind. For many Christians, as long as we have certain people in our lives we are confident we can do what God has called us to do. For others, as long as they have some money in the bank, they are confident they can do what God has told them to do. But the moment those people move on, or the moment the money is no longer in the account, they can feel like it's over. Your world doesn't end when people leave, your world begins! A new chapter begins! That is when you learn how to place your total trust and confidence in the Lord.

When Jesus sent the seventy disciples out two by two, they were commanded not to take anything with them. No money, food, or a change of shoes (see Luke 10:4). What was He doing? Jesus was teaching them how to depend solely on Him. They went out and saw they didn't lack for anything and they experienced great success in ministry.

As you place your total confidence in the Lord, and begin to take forward steps into His purpose and plan, He will bear you up. He will strengthen you. He will cause His grace to abound toward you and you won't lack anything. He will give you great success because your total trust and confidence is in Him. He will cause your walk to turn into a pace, and your pace to turn into a run!

Inspired

I'm inspired
to live out a dream
that wakes me up
causes me to pace
brings tears to my eyes
and fills me with laughter
that which I have been called to
is something I can't shake off
for anything in the world
even if I could
it would find itself
attracted to me
what does it want from me
my dreams tug at me
bother me
until I finally give in
and be myself in Him

A WORD FROM THE LORD

"There is Nothing Too Hard for Me"
July 11, 2016

"I, the Lord, will set things in order for you! I will set you free. I will set your feet on a firm foundation. I will set you on fire for My glory. Don't you see? There's nothing too hard for Me. What I set, none can move. What I set in place and establish by My name, no one can undo. When you turn your heart toward Me, I turn to you. I will establish you in My love and remove all your shame. I will set you free and give you a new name. Sin will not dominate you anymore. Fear won't run your life anymore. Let Me set things in order for you. Set your heart on Me and I will bless you. Set your mind on Me and I will show you great and mighty things you've never known. Will you let Me set you free? Will you let Me set your feet? Will you let Me set you on fire? You are not too hard for Me. Your problem is not too challenging for Me. It's a light thing for Me to deliver you and place you in My perfect will. I will bring you out and bring you in. I

will set you free to be all I made you to be. This is My will for you. Don't you see? This is why, my child, it's not too hard for Me. Like a caterpillar is destined to be a butterfly, nothing can change your destiny in Me. You will be transformed. You will be changed. You will be born anew, and you will walk in all that I prepared for you. I say it again, I will set things in order for you. I will set you free. I will set your feet on a firm foundation. I will set you on fire for Me."

Scripture References: Jeremiah 32:27; Psalms 119:133; Psalms 40:2; Psalms 91:14-16

The Gift of Salvation

When I surrendered my life to the Lord, I didn't understand anything about how to be a "good" Christian, or how to pray, or worship, or even how to study my Bible. All I knew was I had encountered a love that I had never known and a power that I had never experienced before, and I wanted more. As days turned into months and months turned into years, God gradually helped me understand how real my relationship with Him can be. It was no longer my mother or father's relationship with the Lord that I wanted, but I was enjoying my own. It is the real relationship I have with God that has seen me through many, many trials and have made me who I am today.

A real relationship with God begins with a quality decision to let Jesus into your heart and into your life. Your issues and problems don't scare Him. Your fears and anxiety do not move Him. You are His, and He wants to be yours. From the moment He enters into your life, the

Spirit of God roll up His sleeves and go to work in changing you from the inside out.

The Bible tells us in Romans 10:9-10, *"That if you confess with your mouth the Lord Jesus and believe in your heart that God has raised Him from the dead, you will be saved. For with the heart one believes unto righteousness, and with the mouth confession is made unto salvation."*

If you've read this book and you want Jesus to be Lord of your life, pray this prayer from your heart:

Dear Father God, I believe that you sent your Son Jesus to die for my sin. I believe He rose from the dead and is alive today. Dear Lord Jesus, come into my heart. Come into my life and save me now. I repent of sin and turn from it. Thank you for saving me. Change me to look like you on the inside and behave like you on the outside. Be glorified in me. In Jesus' name, Amen.

Renew Your Vow

After a couple has been married for several years, they sometimes experience a dry spell. It's when they go through a season in their relationship when their fire isn't burning as strong as before, and they have allowed other things to enter in and take their minds off of strengthening their marriage. In a similar way, we are in a covenant relationship with God our Father, and while His love always burns passionately for us, sometimes our love for Him wanes. While He has never left us, sometimes we leave His side and drift away. He is always thinking about us more than the number of sand on the seashore, but we can reach a point when He doesn't cross our mind at all during the day (see Psalms 139:17-18).

If this describes your relationship with God, it is time to renew your vow and commitment to Him.
We find in 1 John 1:9, God says, *"If we confess our sins, He is faithful and just to forgive us our sins and to cleanse us from all unrighteousness."* God is

faithful and true, and He is always standing there with open arms, ready to receive us again. He will forgive you and cleanse you of all unrighteousness. He will love you like you never did anything wrong. That's the nature of our God! When you truly understand His love and His grace, you will never want to backslide another day in your life. You'll want to live to please Him because of His unconditional love for you.

Please say this prayer with me if you are ready to renew your vow and commitment to the Father:

Father God, I come to you asking your forgiveness for leaving your side. Forgive me, God. I turn away from sin, and I turn to you. I say "no" to the devil, and I say "yes" to you! I want our relationship to be like it was when I first knew you. Restore me, Lord. I surrender to you completely. Fill me with your Holy Spirit. Help me to love you with all my heart, soul, mind and strength. Let my relationship with you be more important than any other relationship in my life. In Jesus' name, Amen.

The Gift of Holy Spirit

The Bible tells us in Acts 1:8, "But you shall receive power, when the Holy Spirit has come upon you: and you shall be witnesses to Me in Jerusalem, and in all Judea and Samaria, and to the end of the earth." That word power is where we get the word dynamite. However, it's not just a stick of dynamite the Bible is referring to; it's referring to a stick of dynamite that is lit and on fire! When we receive the baptism of the Holy Ghost with the Bible evidence of speaking in other tongues, we become powerful and explosive against the kingdom of darkness. Many times we struggle unnecessarily in our Christian walk because we have no power.

Not only does God want people to be saved and come into His family, but He also wants us to walk in His Holy Ghost power. He wants us to have the total package!

If you desire to receive the Baptism of the Holy Spirit with the Bible evidence of speaking in other tongues, simply pray this prayer out loud from your heart:

Dear Father, I thank you for the gift of your Holy Spirit. I want to walk in your power and anointing. I want to be an effective witness for you. So, Father, I ask that you fill me with your Holy Spirit and come upon me. I receive by faith the baptism of the Holy Spirit with the Bible evidence of speaking with other tongues. Thank you, Lord that I will speak in tongues. In Jesus' name, Amen.

Where Do I Go From Here?

Below are some tips to jumpstart your spiritual walk with God.

Develop a Prayer Life
Prayer is simply communicating with God. In your prayer time, the Holy Spirit can strengthen you, comfort you, encourage you and direct you as you pray for others. Below are Scriptures to help strengthen your prayer life:

- "Do not fret or have any anxiety about anything, but in every circumstance and in everything, by prayer and petition (definite requests), with thanksgiving, continue to make your wants known to God" (Philippians 4:6, AMP).

- "Watch therefore, and pray always that you may be counted worthy to escape all these things that will come to pass, and to stand before the Son of Man" (Luke 21:36, NKJV).

- "Be unceasing in prayer [praying perseveringly]" (1 Thessalonians 5:17, NKJV).

Develop a Word Life

When you read or meditate on the Word of God (the Bible), you will gain more understanding of God's ways and His character, which increases your faith. Your Bible isn't just to sit on the coffee table and collect dust. It is meant to be read and applied in your daily life. Below are Scriptures to help deepen your understanding of God's Word.

- "But he answered and said, "It is written, 'man shall not live by bread alone, but by every word that proceeds from the mouth of God'" (Matthew 4:4, NKJV).

- "As newborn babes, desire the pure milk of the word, that you may grow thereby" (1 Peter 2:2, NKJV).

- "So then faith comes by hearing, and hearing by the word of God" (Romans 10:17, NKJV).

What to do when you feel...

Discouraged

"I called on the LORD in distress; The LORD answered me *and set me* in a broad place." (Psalms 118:5, NKJV).

Fearful

"The LORD *is* my light and my salvation; whom shall I fear? The LORD *is* the strength of my life; Of whom shall I be afraid?" (Psalms 27:1, NKJV).

Additional reference Scriptures: Isaiah 41:13; 2 Timothy 1:7

Tempted

"No temptation has overtaken you except such as is common to man; but God *is* faithful, who will not allow you to be tempted beyond what you are able, but with the temptation will also make the way of escape, that you may be able to bear *it*." (1 Corinthians 10:13, NKJV).

Additional reference Scriptures: 1 John 4:4; James: 1:12; James 4:7

In Need of Wisdom

"If any of you lacks wisdom, let him ask of God, who gives to all liberally and without reproach, and it will be given to him." (James 1:5, NKJV).

Additional reference Scriptures: Proverbs 3:5-7; John 16:13; Proverbs 11:14

Who I Am in Christ Scriptures

It is important that you know who you are in Christ. If you are going to accomplish anything in the earth for God's glory, it will first begin with you knowing who you are in Christ. As you commit to reading the scriptures below, the Lord will reveal to you more and more your true identity in Him!

In whom are hid all the treasures of wisdom and knowledge. (Colossians 2:3)

In whom also ye are circumcised with the circumcision made without hands, in putting off the body of the sins of the flesh by the circumcision of Christ: (Colossians 2:11)

Being justified freely by his grace through the redemption that is in Christ Jesus: (Romans 3:24)

There is therefore now no condemnation to them which are in Christ Jesus, who walk not after the flesh, but after the Spirit. (Romans 8:1)

For the law of the Spirit of life in Christ Jesus hath made me free from the law of sin and death. (Romans 8:2)

Nor height, nor depth, nor any other creature, shall be able to separate us from the love of God, which is in Christ Jesus our Lord. (Romans 8:39)

So we, being many, are one body in Christ, and every one members one of another. (Romans 12:5)

But of him are ye in Christ Jesus, who of God is made unto us wisdom, and righteousness, and sanctification, and redemption: (1Corinthians 1:30)

Now thanks be unto God, which always causeth us to triumph in Christ, and maketh manifest the savour of his knowledge by us in every place. (2Corinthians 2:14)

Therefore if any man be in Christ, he is a new creature: old things are passed away; behold, all things are become new. (2Corinthians 5:17)

To wit, that God was in Christ, reconciling the world unto himself, not imputing their trespasses unto them; and hath committed unto us the word of reconciliation. (2Corinthians 5:19)

For ye are all the children of God by faith in Christ Jesus. (Galatians 3:26)

Blessed be the God and Father of our Lord Jesus Christ, who hath blessed us with all spiritual blessings in heavenly places in Christ: (Ephesians 1:3)

But now in Christ Jesus ye who sometimes were far off are made nigh by the blood of Christ (Ephesians 2:13)

Let this mind be in you, which was also in Christ Jesus: (Philippians 2:5)

For we are the circumcision, which worship God in the spirit, and rejoice in Christ Jesus, and have no confidence in the flesh. (Philippians 3:3)

I press toward the mark for the prize of the high calling of God in Christ Jesus. (Philippians 3:14)

In everything give thanks: for this is the will of God in Christ Jesus concerning you. (1Thessalonians 5:18)

Who hath saved us, and called us with an holy calling, not according to our works, but according to his own purpose and grace, which was given us in Christ Jesus before the world began, (2Timothy 1:9)

Therefore I endure all things for the elect's sakes, that they may also obtain the salvation which is in Christ Jesus with eternal glory. (2Timothy 2:10)

Wherefore thou art no more a servant, but a son; and if a son, then an heir of God through Christ. (Galatians 4:7)

That in the ages to come he might shew the exceeding riches of his grace in his kindness toward us through Christ Jesus. (Ephesians 2:7)

And the peace of God, which passeth all understanding, shall keep your hearts and minds through Christ Jesus. (Philippians 4:7)

I can do all things through Christ which strengtheneth me. (Philippians 4:13)

Make you perfect in every good work to do his will, working in you that which is wellpleasing in his sight, through Jesus Christ; to whom be glory for ever and ever. (Hebrews 13:21)

That the blessing of Abraham might come on the Gentiles through Jesus Christ; that we might receive the promise of the Spirit through faith. (Galatians 3:14)

Likewise reckon ye also yourselves to be dead indeed unto sin, but alive unto God through Jesus Christ our Lord. (Romans 6:11)

For the wages of sin is death; but the gift of God is eternal life through Jesus Christ our Lord. (Romans 6:23)

About the Author

Kesha Trippett is the founder of Daughters of the King International Ministries. She has ministered at women conferences and has counseled, mentored, and discipled many. Possessing a deep passion for inspiring, reviving, and uniting women, Kesha launched Daughters of the King Daily Devotional on October 9, 2012, which is a writing ministry that has experienced phenomenal growth and international reach. She graduated from Georgia Southern University with a Bachelor of Arts degree and a minor in Business Administration. She went on to graduate, with honors, from Word of Faith Bible Training Center and is a licensed minister of the Gospel. She is happily married to her college sweetheart, Bernard Trippett, and is the mother of five great kids: Asia, Bernard, Christian, Daniel, and Ethan—all in ABC order.

Kesha believes in sharing God's Word with power and in a way in which it is easily understood and applied in everyday life. With wisdom well beyond her years, Kesha ministers to women of all ages, race, and backgrounds. She desires for women all over the world to experience the love of God and the reality of His blessings in their lives. When she's not ministering, Kesha can be found enjoying time with her family, painting abstracts, and writing music.

For more information or to schedule Kesha Trippett to speak at your event, please visit www.keshatrippett.com.

Inner Work, Outer Glory

Daughters of the King International Ministries, Inc. are a women's ministry that began on October 9, 2012 by Kesha Trippett. Our mission is to inspire women around the world, to pray for revival among us and to encourage unity. Through our daily devotional ministry, which is *Daughters of the King Daily Devotionals*, we reach hundreds of thousands of readers throughout the world every day. To learn more, visit us online or follow us on our Facebook fan page!

WWW.DOT-K.COM • FACEBOOK.COM/THEDOTKFAMILY

Made in the USA
Columbia, SC
18 June 2017